OBJECT-ORIENTED
PHP
BEST PRACTICES

A Small Handbook of Conventions for
Writing Readable, Sustainable OOPHP Code

Ikram Hawramani

Introduction

This book is written from the perspective of the maintenance programmer. The guy who pays the ultimate price for every single one of your bad decisions. The guy who, after months and months of wading through horrible spaghetti code written over who knows how many years, acquires a cynical sense for what works and what doesn't. He doesn't get excited by the coolest new toys, he wants to write simple, elegant code that will be easy to work with, easy to get into (for newcomers) and easy to change in the future as the project's size grows.

Writing and reading good code is like driving a good car, you forget it is there. While writing and reading bad code is like driving a bad car, it constantly reminds you that it is there. This book is about learning to code in a way that ensures your future self (or the new hire) will be looking down on you amicably, or at least neutrally, instead of boiling with rage at you. "Looking down" because every programmer looks down on every other programmer. Even your future self looks down on you.

By offering real world commandments, I refer to the fact that what sounds good on paper and is taught in textbooks doesn't always translate to the real world. And what feels good when you write it does not mean it will feel good when you edit it or try to build upon it. The goal is to find a balance between theoretical best practices, maintainability and performance.

It is assumed that the reader has a basic knowledge of object-oriented PHP. You should know what a static function is. If not, read a few online tutorials on object-oriented PHP before you start reading this book. It is also assumed that the user interacts with a database on daily basis, though a sufficiently clever reader should be able to generalize the teachings to non-database scenarios.

Table of Contents

1.
How to really think in objects

To illustrate what objects really are, I will start with an example of what objects aren't:

```php
<?php
$person_handler = new PersonHandler();
$person_handler->createPerson($args);
?>
```

The above code shows a common abuse of object oriented concepts. It is basically saying "I don't know what the heck objects are, but I will use them anyway".

Objects are meant to represent "business objects", real or imaginary. An object is meant to represent something within the business problem you are solving, **not** something within the code you are using to solve the problem. Objects have nothing to do with whatever absurd code you are using to manage your code (such as some "person handling module" that the `PersonHandler` class represents). Objects are about the real, non-code items that exist in your problem space, such as "persons", "orders", "files", "cities", and so on.

To know whether your object is really an object or just an abuse of object-oriented code, simply ask yourself this: "Would a non-programmer who is familiar with the business problem I'm trying to solve instantly understand what this object is by reading the variable and class names and nothing else?". To such a person, a `$person_handler` is some magical thing that has no representation within the reality of the problem. Is it some robot the carries people around?

Here is a code snippet that shows objects being used in a sensible manner:

7

```php
<?php
$file = new File($file_id);
$new_file_id = $file->convert('mp4');
$converted_file = new File($new_file_id);
?>
```

The difference here is that the two objects that were instantiated ($file and $converted_file) are both real-world objects. They belong to the business-space of the problem, not the code-space of the code.

The difference, if you look closely, is this: $person_handler refers to itself, it doesn't refer to something outside of itself. While $file and $converted_file refer to *something else* (a real-world file on a disk), they are not self-referential.

In the world of object-oriented programming, we always operate on two planes: The business-space, the *things* that our objects refer to, and the code-space, the actual code that drives the application. Instantiated objects must always represent business-space items (users, sales orders, files, threads, etc.), otherwise they are abuses of object-oriented programming.

When trying to follow the above commandments, you will soon face a problem: If every object must represent a business item, how do you, for example, create new users in a system? No business object has anything to do with user creation. A $user object, which refers to a specific user in the system, cannot create new users. Sometimes this problem is solved using this absurd anti-pattern:

```php
<?php
$user = new User(); // don't pass an ID to
the user class
$user->createUser($args);
?>
```

This doesn't make sense because the $user object here isn't referring to anything at all. It is a ghost whose function is to create new users. It does not refer to a business object. This code abuse creates a

8

dangerous ambiguity: A $user variable in this reality can either refer to real business object, or it can refer to a ghost object. If you are reading a 1000-line file, there is no way to know which of these a $user variable is without scrolling up and finding the instantiation point of the variable.

The solution to the above problems is to use static methods when objects do not make sense

[Note: A function or routine inside a class is called a "method". A function is something that takes an input, operates on it, and returns an output. A routine is something that does something (for example opening a file from disk, or inserting a value inside a database), but whose main task is not to operate on inputs and return outputs (i.e. the main function of routines is their side-effects, rather than their inputs and outputs). Routines are generally called functions, except by purists. In this book I will use the words method and function interchangeably.]

Here is an example:

```php
<?php
$new_user_id = User::create($args);
$new_user = User($new_user_id);
?>
```

We do not need to create a new class for handling users. The User class is sufficient. Use static methods within your class to do things that objects cannot (and should not) do.

One important function of static methods is returning collections of objects. Let's say you need to get a specific set of users based on certain criteria. In such a case you can do something like this:

```php
<?php
$users = User::getUserIdsByGroup($group_id);
?>
```

Sometimes it makes sense to return a collection from an object, as in this case:

```php
<?php
$group = new Group($group_id);
$user_ids = $group->getUserIds();
?>
```

The above case make sense because the users are within that group, so that the $group object is not overstepping its bounds by returning business items that are categorized under it.

Due to the complexity of the real world, sometimes neither an object nor a static function can satisfyingly represent the solution to a problem. Such cases should be dealt with on a case-by-case basis, perhaps after talking to your teammates and finding out what everyone is most comfortable with.

2.
Return IDs instead of objects or rows

Let's say you need to work with an array of students from the Student class:

```php
<?php
$students =
Student::getStudentsInDistrict($district_id)
;
foreach($students as $student) {
  // do stuff
}
?>
```

In such cases, you are faced with a choice. What should the static method Student::getStudentsInDistrict() return? It can return an array of Student objects:

```php
<?php
class Student {
    public static function
getStudentsInDistrict($district_id) {
        $rows = DB::getRows("SELECT id FROM
db.students WHERE district = ?",
$district_id);

        $students_array = [];
        foreach($rows as $row) {
```

```
            $students_array[] = new
Self($row['id']);
        }

        return $students_array;
    }
}
?>
```

While there is nothing wrong with this pattern from an OO perspective, from a real-world practice perspective, it creates unnecessary mental load and makes it harder to edit the code. Let's say you want to make change to how the Student class works, and this requires you to review every usage of the class in your code. If you use the above pattern, you will have absolutely no idea where the Student class is used throughout the pages of your project without searching for *every usage of every single static method of the class.*

Every page that uses getStudentsInDistrict() is using Student objects returned by the Student class. You can search your files for "new Student" to find where the Student class is used. You will also have to search for "getStudentsInDistrict()" (since this method returns Student objects, meaning that the page that contains this method is going to be containing Student objects), and you will have to search for every other method in the Student class that returns Student objects. This is one of those cases where doing the theoretically correct thing can turn your life into a complete nightmare.

But it gets even better. Imagine another class's methods using Student objects and returning them. Now, if you want to make a change to the Student class, you will have to review every usage of "new Student" in your code, every usage of the object-returning static methods in the Student class, and every usage of every static method in other classes that used one of the static methods from the Student class. This can quickly get out of control, and you will find yourself spending hours with five code windows open trying to hold on to a dozen different variables in your head as you work, occasionally staring out the window to wonder what went wrong in your life that prevented you from becoming a gardener.

One way to avoid returning objects is to return the $rows array intact. This is another bad practice, because on the client page (the PHP page that is using the Student class, not a page belonging to an actual business client), there is no way to know the structure of the $rows variable. Is it a flat array or is it two dimensional? If two dimensional, what variables does it contain? Does it just contain IDs like this:

```php
<?php
$rows = [
    ['id' => 5],
    ['id' => 6]
];
?>
```

Or does it contain extra attributes?

```php
<?php
$rows = [
    ['id' => 5, 'first_name' => 'John', ...
],
    ['id' => 6, 'first_name' => 'Sarah',
...]
];
?>
```

You will be forced to review the method inside the class, and sometimes even that is not enough, you have to review the database structure. As a rule, any PHP code that forces you to review the internal data structure of your method or your database is bad code.

The solution to all of these issues is to return IDs from your class's static methods, instead of returning objects or rows:

```php
<?php
class Student {
    public static function
getStudentsInDistrict($district_id) {
        $rows = DB::getRows("SELECT id FROM
db.students WHERE district = ?",
$district_id);

        $student_ids_array =
array_column($rows, 'id');

        return $student_ids_array;
    }
}
?>
```

[Note: The *array_column()* PHP function takes a two-dimensional array and returns a flat array with only the values of the index that is passed to it (in the above example, 'id'). The *$student_ids_array* variable will contain a flat array like *[1, 5, 15]*, each item being the id of a particular student.]

Then, on the client page (remember, "client page" means a page that is a client of the class, i.e. that uses the class) you can instantiate your objects:

```php
<?php
$student_ids =
Student::getStudentsInDistrict($district_id)
foreach($student_ids as $student_id) {
    $student = new Student($student_id);

    // do stuff
}
```

```
?>
```

In this way, if you need to review the usages of Student objects, you merely need to search for "new Student" across your pages and be confident to find every single usage of Student objects. Inside the Student class you'd also need to search for "new Self" as well if there are any methods that instantiate Student objects.

[Note: *Self* refers to the class within which it is used. If you are inside the *Student* class and are instantiating a *Student* object, instead of using *new Student()* you can do *new Self()*. This makes the code more portable, as you can copy it and paste it inside another class, and in the new class *Self* would continue to work as expected, referring to the new class. But if you had used *new Student()*, after pasting the code, you'd need to update it to refer to the new class.]

One issue with always returning IDs is performance, as getting the IDs would require one database call, and instantiating the objects on the client page would require additional database calls. This is mostly mitigated by using the caching methods that will be described later in the book. Thanks to the extreme speed of today's disks, networks and processors, if you use the caching methods that will covered, performance would only be a worry if you are dealing with tens of thousands of objects. In such cases you can selectively choose to return rows from the database onto the page.

In my experience of maintaining an educational system of 450,000 lines with thousands of users, returning IDs makes sense in 99% of cases. Returning anything besides IDs should be a rare case of extreme tuning, similar to writing high-hit-rate parts of a video game engine in assembly.

15

3.
Most constructors should only take one argument

Here is an example of a bad constructor:

```php
<?php
class Student {
    public function __construct($id,
$first_name, $last_name) {

        // content
    }
}
?>
```

This is bad because it assumes that the client page that is calling this constructor will have the $first_name and $last_name variables available to it, which is not guaranteed. It is not good practice to force the calling page to get data from a secondary source before it calls the class that is supposed to have the data.

The constructor could be changed so that it takes $first_name and $last_name variables while allowing you to call it without providing the variables:

```php
<?php
$student = new Student($id, null, null);
?>
```

This is bad for two reasons. It complicates the usage of the class, so that everyone who instantiates a Student object will have to remember that it takes two extra arguments. Some programmers may start using the class as follows:

```php
<?php
$student = new Student($id);
?>
```

This works since the other two variables are optional. But then other programmers will start using this as the default, meaning that the constructor's additional arguments may become nothing more than unnecessary maintenance overhead.

Another issue is that letting a constructor take extra arguments gives these arguments a special status that they do not necessarily deserve. Why shouldn't we also pass the constructor the student's date of birth, zip code, guardian name or any other number of possible attributes? Generally the extra arguments are chosen arbitrarily and according to the needs of the moment, and even after they lose relevance, they often continue to be a drag on the class's maintenance for the rest of its lifetime.

The best solution, then, is to have a convention to only allow one argument to the constructor, generally the database ID that identifies the object, except in rare circumstances where more arguments are necessary. For example, sometimes an object requires two variables to be identified, in such cases allowing two arguments is necessary.

4.
Don't instantiate objects unless you know they exist

When doing object-oriented programming, in many, or most, cases you have an ID that you use to instantiate an object.

```php
<?php
$student = new Student($id);
?>
```

But sometimes an object-oriented concept doesn't have a specific ID associated with it, for example:

```php
<?php
$student_lunch = new
StudentLunch($student_id, $date);
?>
```

In such cases, there is often the temptation to do something like this:

```php
<?php
$student_lunch = new
StudentLunch($student_id, $date);
If($student_lunch->exists()) {
  // check if the student lunch has already been
  // recorded
}
```

```
else {
   // record the lunch

}
?>
```

This practice reduces productivity and creates a potentially dangerous ambiguity in your code. You never know if an object really represents something, or if it is a hollow container that could potentially refer to nothing. For every long piece of code you read, you'd have to scroll up to find the object's instantiation point to find out whether there is a check to ensure that the object is really an object or whether it has to be created. And if during a long day of coding you forget to add that check to the code you write, this could lead to bugs that are potentially difficult to fix.

The solution is to never construct an object unless you know it really exists. In the case of the student lunch, you'd do as follows:

```
<?php
if(!StudentLunch::hasBeenRecorded($student_id, date)) {
   StudentLunch::recordLunch($student_id, $date)
}
$student_lunch = new StudentLunch($student_id, $date);
?>
```

The issue could also exist even if there is a single ID identifying the object. For example let's say you've been tasked with creating some horrible local social network for a college. To instantiate a student profile, you'd do as follows:

```
<?php
$student_profile = new StudentProfile($student_id);
```

```
?>
```

We have no guarantee that a profile exists for this student. The easy solution would be to use the `exists()` function mentioned earlier, which adds the harmful ambiguity mentioned. The good solution is to enforce the convention that all objects that are instantiated must exist, and that checking for whether an object exists should be done with static function, *not* with object methods, since once you've instantiated an object, you've already implied that it exists, so it is an abuse of object-oriented programming to add a check for existence *after* you've instantiated the object.

```php
<?php
If(StudentProfile::profileExists($student_id
) {
    // instantiate object.
}
else {
    die('Sorry, but the profile you are trying
to view does not exist.');
}
?>
```

5.

Classes must never return objects belonging to other classes

In a previous chapter, I mentioned that the best convention for avoiding maintenance headaches when dealing with OO code is to always return IDs from a class's static functions, instead of returning database rows or instantiated objects. But you may not be able to convince your teammates to abide by this convention, or your manager may prevent you from doing things this way. In such cases, here is a less strict convention that will ensure things do not go completely out of hand.

Having a class return objects from another class creates a horrible dependency chain (as I've explained earlier). If you have a bunch of functions in a `District` class that returns `Student` objects from the `Student` class, whenever you want to make a change to the `Student` class, you will be forced to update the `Student` class, the `District` class, and every page that uses either the `Student` class or the `District` class's static functions.

The best way to prevent such situations is to prevent classes from returning objects. The second best way is to prevent classes from returning objects belonging to other classes.

Note that it is fine for a class to use objects belonging to other classes, as long it does not *return* the objects. For example this is perfectly fine:

```php
<?php
class Student {
    public function getDistrictId() {
        $school = new School($student-
>getSchoolId());

        return $school->getDistrictId();
    }
}
?>
```

The above code initializes a School object inside the Student class. This is not a problem since the School object is not being returned. The function simply uses the School object to perform some operation, then returns a number.

This is fine because the Student class simply becomes yet another client of the School class. There are no secondary pages involves in some chain-of-dependency, so changing the School class will not force you to review every usage of Student->getDistrictId() in the system. You only need to review this one function, the same way you'd review any other piece of code that uses the School class.

6.
Never create nested objects

Nested objects are objects that are put inside another object. This is a subset of the case covered in the previous chapter (classes returning objects belonging to other classes), but it deserves its own chapter because of how bad it is. For example:

```php
<?php
class Student {
    public static function loadStudent($id)
{
        $student = new Self($id);
        $student->exam_results = new
ExamResult($id);
        $student->address = new
Address($id);

        // down the rabbit hole we go
        // where it stops we do not know
    }
}
?>
```

And it is used this way:

```php
<?php
$student = Student::loadStudent($id);
foreach($student->examp_results as
$exam_result) {
```

```
  $exam_result->some_other_object-
>do_something();
}
?>
```

This is one of those absolutely horrible practices that seem like a good idea to a certain type of programmer who thinks just because the language allows you to do it, it must be a good idea.

As it should be clear from previous chapters, this is bad because it makes it unclear where objects belonging to particular classes are used. If you want to update ExamResult, you will also have to review every function inside every other class that nests this object as part of their own object.

Another reason it is bad is because such large, monolithic objects create a steep learning curve for new programmers joining the team, as they would need to become familiar with a dozen classes before they can clearly understand what is going on a simple code page.

Some of the most difficult work I've done in my life as a programmer is refactoring nested objects. One system I worked on had a User class that loaded objects from about a dozen other classes into its own objects. And some of these classes also loaded objects from other classes into their objects. This object (and a few other similar ones) were creating a performance bottleneck on the system, since doing something as simple as getting a user's full name requires a User object, which did about 50 unnecessary database calls every time it was instantiated thanks to all the objects nested within it.

7.
Use a loadMeta() function to load data only when you need it

In the example below, we have a Student class that offers three public methods besides its constructor, a getId() method that simply returns the ID that we pass to the constructor, and two methods (getFullName() and getZipCode()) that retrieve data from the database and return it.

```php
<?php
class Student {
    private $id;
    private $first_name;
    private $last_name;
    private $zip_code;

    public function __construct($id) {
        $this->id = $id;
    }
    public function getId() {
        return $this->id; // doesn't need a
database call
    }

    public function getFullName() {
      // needs a database call
    }
```

27

```php
    public function getZipCode() {
        // needs a database call
    }
}
?>
```

Some coders write a separate database query for each function that needs the database. But this is bad for two reasons. It increases database load as every function has to make a new request for the data it needs. And it creates maintenance load as every function's database queries have to be separately maintained.

There are various ways of solving this problem. My favorite solution is something simple, lean and easy to learn and use. It is to create a function called `loadMeta()` that retrieves data for all the functions that need it once one of the functions that need it are called.

[Note: I chose the name "loadMeta" since it has something to do with the class (i.e. it is a "meta" function, rather than a client function), and it doesn't sound scary or magical like "__load" would sound to a newbie. My colleagues went along with the name without complaining, so it probably isn't a terrible name, even if it is a slight abuse of the word "meta". But you are free to name it anything you want.]

Here is some code to illustrate the concept:

```php
<?php
class Student {
    private $id;
    private $first_name;
    private $last_name;
    private $zip_code;
    private $meta_loaded = false;

    public function __construct($id) {
```

```php
        $this->id = $id;
    }
    public function getId() {
        return $this->id; // doesn't need a
database call
    }

    public function getFullName() {
      $this->loadMeta();

      return $this->first_name . ' ' .
$this->last_name;
    }

    public function getZipCode() {
      $this->loadMeta();

      return $this->zip_code;
    }

    private function loadMeta() {
        if($this->meta_loaded) {
            return;
        }
        $this->meta_loaded = true;

        $row = DB::getRow("SELECT * FROM
table ... WHERE id = ?", $this->getId());

        $this->first_name =
$row['first_name'];
        $this->last_name =
$row['last_name'];
```

29

```
        $this->zip_code = $row['zip_code'];
    }
}
?>
```

The loadMeta() function is only called once. When the first method that needs a database call is called (for example getZipCode()), it calls loadMeta() first, which pre-fills the $zip_code variable AND two other variables ($first_name and $last_name), then returns the variable.

Next, if you call getFullName(), it calls loadMeta(), but it immediately returns, since the $meta_loaded variable has been set to true. No database call is made, the function returns the $first_name and $last_name variables that were pre-filled by the earlier call to getZipCode().

[Note: DB::getRow() is a wrapper function for running prepared SQL statements while avoiding writing repetitive boilerplate code. This will be further discussed in a later chapter.]

[Note: Notice how I set the $meta_loaded variable to true right on the fourth line of the loadMeta() function. Theoretically it makes more sense to set this variable to true at the end of the function. But in practice, too many times I saw that I (or someone else) forgot to set it true at the end, meaning that the whole point of the function was lost as all the class methods were making repeated database calls. For this reason we decided to set it true at the beginning to avoid forgetting doing so at the end. We soon learned to recognize this as a pattern; every loadMeta() function in the project had these four lines at the beginning, a check and a setting of $meta_loaded to true.]

Ideally, each class is only related to a single table in the database, so that a single loadMeta() call is sufficient to retrieve every variable the class needs without having to do joins. However, in some cases, a few of the methods in a class require access to a second table, or access to a different row in the same table. In such cases a separate loadMeta() should be created. For example:

```
public function getZipCode() {

    $this->loadMeta();

    return $this->zip_code;
}

    public function
getInstructor($subject_id) {
        $this->loadInstructorMeta();

        return $this-
>instructors[$subject_id];
    }

    private function loadInstructorMeta() {
        if($this->instructor_meta_loaded) {
            return;
        }
        $this->instructor_meta_loaded =
true;

        // do db calls, fill the
$instructors array
        // and any other relevant variables
with data from db
    }
```

In the above example, the new method getInstructor() is added to the Student class. This function gets its data from another table

31

(not the table where the student's personal data is stored, for example there might be a db.students and a db.si_map). We create a new loadMeta() function for getting data for functions that need this table, calling it loadInstructorMeta(). The getInstructor() method relies on this meta function to get its data. Other methods can be added to the class that also rely on loadInstructorMeta().

Using this design, Student objects can be used where they are needed while only hitting the database when necessary. A student's ID can be retrieved without making any database calls. Their zip code can be retrieved without hitting the instructors table. Their instructors can be retrieved without hitting the student's personal data table.

8.
Put exceptions everywhere

Exceptions are error messages for developers, as opposed to the users of the system. They are there to prevent yourself and other developers from introducing errors into the system that are only caught months or years later when someone else reviews the code.

Developers may be reluctant to use exceptions due to the fear of having to worry about catching the exception (using a throw and catch pattern). But in web applications catching exceptions is generally not necessary. In web applications, exceptions are used as a more developer-friendly alternative to die(), since exception messages provide helpful debugging data, such as the line of code of the page that led to the exception.

Since exceptions cause the page to fail to load properly, the developer will have to deal with them before moving on to doing something else, meaning that they cannot be ignored and bad code will not be left inside the codebase for long.

```php
<?php
if($newbie_programmer_doesnt_know_what_on_ea
rth_they_are_doing) {
        throw new Exception('crash and burn,
baby!');
}
?>
```

In your class methods, use exceptions to make it easy to catch bad usages of methods:

```php
<?php
    public function __construct($id) {
        if(!is_numeric($id) || $id < 1) {
            throw new Exception('Bad ID: ' .
$id);
        }

        $this->id = $id;
    }
?>
```

The above example is the constructor of the Student class updated to catch cases where the $id variable is not supplied properly.

```php
<?php
$id = $_POST['id'];
$student = new Student($id);
?>
```

In the above example, due to an error in HTML or JavaScript, the $_POST['id'] variable may not be set, or set to an improper value (such as an empty string). Having the exception in the Student class constructor enables you to immediately see the error without wasting your time hunting for why the page doesn't work as expected:

Exception message: Bad id:

GET:
[ ]

POST:
[ ]

Stack Trace:

```
#0
/var/www/html/somedir/client_page.php(25):
Student->__construct()
```

The above exception message tells you that the **Student->__construct()** function failed due to a bad ID being passed to it on line 25 of **client_page.php**.

To see the above information when exceptions occur, you need to enable the displaying of PHP errors, and then you will need to add a function like this to your bootstrap file (the file that is included with every page of the project, which initiates DB connections, creates sessions, etc.) so that it is available on all pages:

```
set_exception_handler(
    function ($exception) {
        $exceptionMessage = $exception->getMessage();
        $getJson = json_encode($_GET,
JSON_PRETTY_PRINT);
        $postJson = json_encode($_POST,
JSON_PRETTY_PRINT);
        $stackTrace = $exception->getTraceAsString();

        $body = "<pre>Exception message:
$exceptionMessage<br><br>
                GET:<br>$getJson<br><br>
                POST:<br>$postJson<br><br>
                Stack
Trace:<br>$stackTrace</pre>";

        echo $body;
    }
);
```

9.
Have an Assert class

An Assert class makes it easier to add exceptions where they are needed. Instead of manually checking for exception conditions, as follows:

```php
public function __construct($id) {
    if(!is_numeric($id) || $id < 1) {
        throw new Exception('Bad ID: ' .
$id);
    }

    $this->id = $id;
}
```
You can instead do this:

```php
<?php
public function __construct($id) {
    Assert::isId($id);

    $this->id = $id;
}
?>
```

And your Assert class can look like this:

```php
<?php
class Assert {
    public static function isId($input) {
        if(!is_numeric($input) || $input <
1) {
            throw new Exception('Bad id: ' .
$input);
        }
    }
}
?>
```

This way, you write the exception check only once, in the Assert class, and then you are able to use it everywhere.

Name the arguments to Assert functions $input, this reinforces the practice of treating input with suspicion. If you named the variable $id, it would give the argument a veneer of legitimacy, when the whole point of the Assert class is to treat input as guilty until proven innocent.

10.
Have an autoloader

An autoloader is merely a few lines of code that helps your PHP pages find classes without you having to include or require them on the page. Having to worry about where class files are located, and remembering to include the correct ones on a page, is a big annoyance and it reduces your productivity. An autoloader does it all for you. Here is an example autoloader that you can include in your bootstrap file:

```php
<?php
spl_autoload_register(function ($class) {
    $file = __DIR__ .
'/somepath/classes_directory/' . $class .
'.class.php';
    if(file_exists($file)) {
        require_once $file;
    }
});
```

[Note: *spl_autoload_register()* is a special PHP function for creating autoloaders.]

The above example assumes that your class files are located in project_path/somepath/classes_directory, that the file names are exactly the same as the class names, and that they all end in ".class.php". For example a Student class's file would be named Student.class.php   (not   student.class.php   or Student.php).

Now, you will be able to write $student = new Student($id); wherever you want without including or requiring the class file. All you will need to do is include the bootstrap file once at the top of the page, and from there all your classes will be available to you.

The autoloader only includes classes that are required by the page, it doesn't include every single class in your classes directory as you might fear.

Note that with this setup you can only have one class per file, which is great, since having multiple classes per file is bad practice and shouldn't be allowed.

11.
Make everything private, unless there is a very good reason to make them public

This chapter is about using proper (fanatical) encapsulation. If you know what that is, you can skip the chapter.

Private variables and methods are those that can only be accessed within the class (only within the code that is enclosed by the class's braces):

```php
<?php
class Student {
    private $id;

    private function loadMeta() {
        //
    }
}

// Student->id and Student->loadMeta()
cannot be used or accessed here outside of
the braces
?>
```

Making a variable private prevents it from being directly accessed from a client page. Direct access to a class's properties ("properties" is the PHP name for a class's variables) looks like this:

```php
<?php
$student = new Student($id);
$student->loadData();
echo $student->first_name . ' ' . $student->last_name;

foreach($student->instructors as $instructor_id) {
    // ,
} ?>
```

The above code is using the **$first_name**, **$last_name** and **$instructors** variables of the class outside of the class. This makes the class's data structures vulnerable to being corrupted. For example let's say a programmer writes this buggy code:

```php
<?php
foreach($all_student_ids as $student_id) {
    $student = new Student($student_id);

    if($student->school_id = '55') {
        // say goodbye to your database
    }
}
?>
```

Notice that the **if** clause is actually assigning the value '55' to the variable **$school_id**, instead of checking if the value of **$school_id** equals '55'. This means that if the code is meant to delete every student account in the school with the id of '55', it will actually delete every single account in the system regardless of the school id, since the **if** clause always returns true.

Another very serious problem with using class variables on client pages is that client pages become dependent on the class's internal data structure, so that you cannot change the class's internal structure without random client pages breaking.

Now, you might be clever enough to avoid situations where you loop over every user (or invoice, or order) in the system, but can you trust your colleagues to be as careful? What about some random new guy hired by HR without your input?

By making class variables private, this type of vulnerability can be prevented. Instead of allowing outside code to access variables, create methods that give access to the data as needed. For example instead of letting client code access $school_id, have a getSchoolId() function:

```php
public function getSchoolId() {
    $this->loadMeta();

    return $this->school_id;
}
```

If the code in the previous example had used such a method, it would have instantly crashed without doing damage:

```php
<?php
foreach($all_student_ids as $student_id) {
    $student = new Student($student_id);

    if($student->getSchoolId() = '55') { //
fatal error
        // nothing bad happens
    }
}
?>
```

Using private methods instead of public methods offers similar benefits. There is no reason for the `loadMeta()` function (described in a previous chapter) to be public, for example. Certain methods might cause dangerous side-effects if they are used outside of the class in the wrong place and time.

By making private your default, if a newbie programmer tries to abuse a method by using it on a client page when it is not supposed to be used as such, they will get a fatal error and will be forced to learn the proper usage of the method.

This idea of managing access to your class variables and methods is called encapsulation. A class's variables and methods should all be private, except for a very specific set of public methods that provide the public API for the class. These public methods provide a safe and controlled way of letting yourself and other developers use the class.

Think of your classes as nuclear bunkers where communication with the outside world can only be done through a few safe routes. How the inside of the bunker works should mean nothing to people outside of the bunker. Rearranging the furniture inside the bunker should not cause a power outage in a neighboring town. And the happiness of the people in the neighboring town should not rely on how you arrange the contents of your fridge.

It is a good idea to use getter methods inside the class itself too (not just outside of the class), as this prevents data corruption, and it helps your functions become less dependent on the data structures used by other functions.

12.
Have unbypassable authoritative classes for interacting with your business objects

Let's say you have a `Student` class that you use to interact with a `students` table in your database. Having random PHP pages that do their own queries on the `students` table (without using the `Student` class) creates massive maintenance headaches. For example if you want to format the way student names appear in the system, instead of being able to just make a change to `Student->getFullName()`, you will be forced to search for all queries in the system that retrieve data from the `students` table and update every one of them that retrieve a first name and last name.

Another issue with having random pages bypass the class is that it makes your tables "sticky", you will not be able to make changes to your database without having random stuff break (often without you knowing about it). If you have a single authoritative class that handles all interactions with the `student` table, as long as you update the class, you can be sure that nothing out of the class breaks.

Yet one more issue with not having authoritative classes is if you want to implement caching. By having a single authoritative class for a business object, you can implement the caching inside the class and know that everywhere the caching will now apply. But if random pages bypass the class, they will also bypass the cache.

Yet another issue is bypassing the MySQL query cache (and similar caches). Having a single authoritative class for retrieving information means that MySQL can cache queries effectively. Having random pages do their own queries means that repetitive queries will be made without being cached, since even a single space difference between two queries that are exactly the same otherwise makes MySQL treat them as different queries, so that if MySQL caches one of the queries, it will have no benefit for the other query, even though both queries request the same data.

Once you try to implement the commandments of this chapter, you will face the problem of having to deal with pages that need joined data from two or more tables, but where each table has its own authoritative class. This is usually an issue with reports pages, as reports often need joined data from various tables. One way to deal with such situations is to have hybrid classes, such as `StudentInstructorAuthority`, `StudentInstructorMediator`, or any other name that your team likes. This class will hold all methods that pull data from the `students` AND `instructors` tables.

Now, you can go crazy with this and have classes with the names of six tables in the class name. Instead of this, you could create a class with the database's name in its name that handles all multi-table data pulling operations, for example `SMSMediator` (assuming your database is called "sms", short for "School Management System"). At the place I work, we simply decided to stop fussing about pages that did multi-table queries, allowing them to exist the way they were, as most of them were reports that were accessed a few times a year.

It is a judgment call. If you see the same three tables being called from various pages, it might make sense to create a class for them. Other times, creating classes for such pages might create maintenance overhead without contributing significant value.

13.
Reuse objects with a global repository class to avoid duplicate database hits

This chapter is about reusing objects during a page's execution to improve performance (it is not about reusing objects between different page loads). This is especially valuable for loops that instantiate objects. Imagine a situation like this:

```php
<?php
foreach($all_student_ids_in_district as
$student_id) {
  $student = new Student($student_id);

  $school = new School($student-
>getSchoolId());

  $school_name = $school->getName();

  // and so on
}
?>
```

Let's say the variable $all_student_ids_in_district holds the ids of 2000 students belonging to 10 schools, so that we have 200 students per school. The above loop instantiates a School object for each student.

47

The problem should be obvious, as there are 200 students that share the same school, re-instantiating a School object for each student is a massive waste of resources, as ideally we would only retrieve the school's data once, and reuse the data for all the students who belong to the same school.

Cases like the above were the main reason my team was hesitant to go all-in with object-oriented practices. One solution was to implement a caching mechanism inside each class that detected duplicate calls for objects and retrieved them from memory, as follows:

```
private static $cache = []; // "static"
so that it sticks around

public static function get($id) {
    if(!isset($cache[$id])) {
        $cache[$id] = new Self($id);
    }

    return $cache[$id];
}

public function __construct($id) {
    Assert::isId($id);

    $this->id = $id;
}
```

To use the cache, instead of doing $school = new School($id), you would do $school = School::get($id). The get() function checks if the object has already been instantiated before, in which case it returns the object from the $cache variable, otherwise it instantiates the object, stores it in the $cache variable for future use, then returns it.

[Note: Since in PHP objects are passed by reference, not by value, the $cache variable will not be holding copies of the objects, it will simply hold references to the real objects, preventing them from being destroyed by the PHP garbage collector during the page's execution. This means that the $cache variable will not be a big bloated variable, it will be quite small, merely holding IDs and pointers to the location of the objects in memory. Its function is merely to "hold onto" the objects so that they do not go away.]

With the above implemented in the School class, we can now do this:

```php
<?php
foreach($all_student_ids_in_district as
$student_id) {
  $student = new Student($student_id);

  $school = School::get($student-
>getSchoolId());

  $school_name = $school->getName();

  // and so on
}
?>
```

Now, the School object is being instantiated only once per school, and then reused for each student that belongs to that particular school. This means that a maximum of only 10 school objects will be created throughout the loop's lifetime (since there are only 10 schools in the district as described earlier).

The problem with this method is that my team decided it was too much of an annoyance to implement a separate cache for each class. There had to be a better way.

After months of thinking, during a caffeine and phenylpiracetam fueled 15-minutes of clarity, I wrote the following class:

```php
<?php
class Repository {
    private static $repository = [];

    public static function get($class_name,
$id) {

        if(!isset(self::$repository[$class_n
ame][$id])) {
            self::$repository[$class_name][$
id] = new $class_name($id);
        }

        return
self::$repository[$class_name][$id];
    }
}
?>
```

The class **Repository** could now be used to cache objects belonging to *any* class without modifying our classes at all. The previous loop can now be modified to this:

```php
<?php
foreach($all_student_ids_in_district as
$student_id) {
  $student = new Student($student_id);

  $school = Repository::get('School',
$student->getSchoolId());

  $school_name = $school->getName();

  // and so on
```

```
}
?>
```

The get() function of the Repository class requires a class name and an ID. The class name is used to dynamically instantiate an object from the class using the $id that is passed as its second argument.

Using the Repository class, object caching could be implemented across the whole system with barely any downsides. We quickly updated a lot of pages to use it, often speeding up pages by a factor of 5-10.

One downside is its strange and ugly syntax. Another issue was that it broke our IDE's autocomplete feature as the IDE could no longer tell what class the $school object belonged to. This was solved by adding a class hint comment above the line where the Repository::get() function is used, as follows:

```php
<?php
/** @var School $school */
$school = Repository::get('School',
$student->getSchoolId());
?>
```

That special comment tells your IDE that the $school variable belongs to the School class. This is the syntax used by the PhpStorm IDE, others might use a different syntax.

Using caching with the *new* statement

If you (or your team) don't like the idea of using a get() function to create objects instead of using the universal new Class() statement, there is a way to continue using the new statement while also making use of the Repository class, as follows:

```php
public function __construct($user_id) {
```

```php
        if(Repository::isCached(self::class,
func_get_args()[0])) {
            foreach
(get_object_vars(Repository::get(self::class
, func_get_args()[0])) as $key => $value) {
                $this->$key = $value;
            }
        }
        else {
            // normal constructor code
        }
        Repository::store(self::class,
func_get_args()[0], $this);
    }
```

[Note: The *Repository::isCached()* and
Repository::store() methods will be talked about later below.]

The above is an update to a typical constructor that first checks if the object has already been cached in the past. If so, it copies all the values from the old object into the new one, meaning that while a new object is created by the constructor, the new object will come with its variables pre-filled, so that it won't need to make any database calls to return data.

The above code can be copied and pasted into any constructor without making any other change to the class, as it uses special PHP functionalities like **self::class** and **func_get_args()** to make it independent of the class it is being used in. Only the "else" part of the code has to be updated, here is where the code from the old constructor is kept.

At the end of the constructor, there is a call to **store()** which updates the cached object in the repository, regardless of whether a new object has been instantiated, or whether the constructor reused an old object. This is to deal with cases where you use an object without using any of its methods that pull data from the database. Once this object is cached (as it will be with the above constructor), reusing it will have no benefit since it doesn't help you save database calls. By always storing the latest object, as an object's methods are called and its variables filled, the cached object will always have the completest version of the object.

[Note: Property copying requires every property of your class to be *protected* rather than *private*. This is not usually an issue as protected properties have the same benefits as private properties. It is only an issue if you have a lot of inheritance going on, which you shouldn't, as will be talked about in a later chapter.]

There are various issues with this approach, however. For one thing, you will need to update every constructor of every class to make use of it.

For another, this is not object re-use exactly, this is the copying of object properties, which is slower. I did tests with 30,000 object instantiations that made use of the database, here are the results I got: With the MySQL query cache disabled, and no object reuse, the test took 1.1 seconds. With the MySQL query cache enabled, it took 427 milliseconds (0.427 seconds). With property copying (the method described right above), the test took 30 milliseconds. With using the `Repository` class directly (through the `Repository::get()` method as described earlier in the chapter) the test took 1.26 milliseconds. So property copying is about 24 times slower than using the Repository class directly. But it is at least 14 times faster than not using it at all and relying on the MySQL query cache alone. While it is not as fast as using the `Repository` class directly, it is still quite a valuable improvement over having no caching at all.

Yet another issue is that in some rare cases objects can get outdated. You may update a student's address, but if their object is cached, doing new `Student($id)` will create an object that has the student's old address if the address has already been prefilled previously. In these cases a `Repository::forget()` function is needed to clear the object from the cache.

Another issue is that using the `new` statement and getting cached object values may not feel intuitive to everyone, even though to me it is not an issue.

Below is what the `isCached()`, `store()` and `forget()` functions of the Repository class look like:

```
    public static function
isCached($class_name, $id) {
        if(isset(self::$repository[$class_na
me][$id])) {
            return true;
        }
        return false;
    }

    public static function
store($class_name, $id, $object) {
        self::$repository[$class_name][$id]
= $object;
    }

    public static function
forget($class_name, $id) {
        unset(self::$repository[$class_name]
[$id]);
    }
```

Conclusion

On my team, we decided to use `$object = new Class($id);` without implementing any caching in the constructor, and we decided to use the `Repository::get()` function only in situations where performance was needed (such as in loops where some objects could get reinstantiated). On most of our PHP pages objects were instantiated once and used throughout the page without reinstantiation, meaning that getting the object from the `Repository` class provided no additional performance benefit. But on certain pages objects were being reinstantiated, so we used the `Repository` class there for those objects that got reinstantiated (while continuing to use the new statement even on those pages, for objects that weren't getting reinstantiated), in certain cases speeding up pages from taking 10 seconds to load to taking 0.5 seconds.

This way we got performance improvements where we needed them with minimum overhead, minimum upkeep, and minimum code modification.

14.
Best inheritance is no inheritance

Inheritance is one of those OO ideas that sound good in theory, that sound good to a beginner, and that sound good to your boss, but that can turn your life into utter misery when misused.

Having inheritance means having to keep track of two different classes while using one object. It creates additional, often unnecessary, mental load during your everyday programming. There are a few cases where inheritance makes sense. For example, you can have a User class which contains all the basic capabilities a user object needs. You can then create Student and Instructor classes that inherit their basic functionalities from it, and also contain functionalities specific to students or instructors.

In a real project, such situations where inheritance makes perfect sense are quite rare and quite obvious. It is fine to use inheritance there. But don't think of inheritance as a cure-all. Having more than one level of inheritance will require you to keep track of three classes at once, a feat that most human brains aren't capable of for any significant stretch of time. When you write the classes yourself, it might seem easy and natural to use even four levels of inheritance. The problem is when someone else has to understand and update your code. This can easily turn into a nightmare with the programmer having to keep track of three or four different windows of code at once, and unable to change anything without random bugs cropping up all over the place.

For this reason, as a rule, inheritance must be treated with extreme suspicion and extreme caution. Think of inheritance as something that doubles the mental load of maintenance work for each level of inheritance (meaning that having three levels of inheritance, i.e. four classes in an inheritance hierarchy, would increase the mental load of maintenance by a factor of 8. 8 and above is what I call suicidal ideation territory for the maintenance programmer(s)). If the benefits offered by the inheritance clearly outweigh this added load, then it is fine to use it. Otherwise do not use it.

15.
Use a database wrapper class for doing prepared statements

Prepared statements are the only acceptable way of interacting with a database. Using prepared statements reduces your change of suffering an SQL injection attack to nearly zero. It also helps prevent accidentally corrupting the database. It also helps you easily catch bugs in your code and queries by throwing exceptions.

A normal SQL query in PHP looks like this (using the MySQLi class):

```php
<?php
$response = $mysqli->query("SELECT * FROM
db.students WHERE id = {$id}");
$row = $response->fetch_assoc();
?>
```

While a query with a prepared statement looks like this:

```php
<?php
$statement = $mysqli->prepare("SELECT * FROM
db.students WHERE id = ?");
$statement->bind_param('i', $id);
$statement->execute();
$response = $statement->get_result();
$row = $response->fetch_assoc();
?>
```

Having to use five lines of code is a really bloated way of getting a row from the database, which is why sometimes programmers are hesitant to use prepared statements. But by using a simple database wrapper class, which I will call DB, these five lines can be turned into one simple and intuitive statement:

```php
<?php
$row = DB::getRow('SELECT * FROM db.students
WHERE id = ?', $id);
?>
```

This is a beautiful productivity enhancer that provides you with the benefits of prepared statements while also helping you avoid annoying bugs like forgetting to do a `$statement->execute();` during your prepared query.

Here is what the DB::getRow() and its parent, DB::getRows() look like:

```php
    public static function getRow($sql,
$param_or_params = null) {
        $rows = DB::getRows($sql,
$param_or_params);
        if(!empty($rows)) {
            return $rows[0];
        }
        else {
            return false;
        }
    }


    public static function getRows($sql,
$param_or_params = null) {
```

```php
        $stmt = self::mysqli()-
>prepare($sql);

        if ($param_or_params) {
            if (is_array($param_or_params))
{
                $args = [str_repeat('s',
count($param_or_params))] ;
                foreach ($param_or_params as
&$value) {
                    $args[] = $value;
                }
            }
            else {
                $args = ['s',
&$param_or_params] ;
            }

            $ref = new
ReflectionClass($stmt);

            $res = $ref-
>getMethod('bind_param')->invokeArgs($stmt,
$args);
        }

        $res = $stmt->execute();
        $res = $stmt->get_result();
        $rows = $res-
>fetch_all(MYSQLI_ASSOC);

        return $rows;
```

```
        }
```

[Note: Various error-checking clauses can be added to the above function.]

The above functions do a lot of magical looking stuff if you are not used to references and `Reflection` classes. But you don't need to worry about how it works, as it just works. If you do want to find out how it works, some web searching should be sufficient. For example you can read the various user comments on the PHP manual page for `mysqli_stmt::bind_param` where people discuss their own takes on creating DB wrapper classes.

The `DB::getRow()` and `DB::getRows()` functions can take scalars and arrays. Here are three usage examples:

```php
<?php
$row = DB::getRow('SELECT * FROM x WHERE y =
? AND z = ?', [$a, $b]);
$rows = DB::getRows($some_sql, $some_id);
$row = DB::getRow($sql);
?>
```

One small issue with using these functions is that `DB::getRows()` assumes all parameters are strings, so you cannot rely on it to catch errors where you pass a textual string for a database column that can only accept numbers. What this means is that you will have to do any error checking in the PHP code that calls `getRows()`. My team thought this was perfectly fine as we never relied on prepared statements to check our data integrity.

The `getRows()` function, however, can be updated to take a parameter type string as another argument, for example so that it can be used like this:

```php
<?php
```

```
$row = DB::getRow('SELECT * FROM x WHERE y =
? AND z = ?', 'si', [$a, $b]);
?>
```

In this example, the `'si'` string tells MySQL that the first parameter is a string and the second parameter is an integer. This is how our `getRows()` function originally was, but we decided to get rid of this parameter type argument to simplify its usage.

Using the above code as inspiration, you can now create new wrapper functions such as `DB::insert('db.tablename', ['col_name' => value, 'col2_name' => value])` and `DB::updateRow('db.tablename', ['col_name' => value, 'col2_name' => value])` that do not require passing an SQL query at all.

You can also create a `DB::execute()` function for doing SQL queries whose return values you do not need. You could, in theory, use `DB::getRows()` for this, but this gives the function a double-meaning (it "overloads" its purpose) which is generally bad practice, as it will require double mental effort to read the code to find out whether a value is being retrieved or whether a query is being executed with no need for a return value. `DB::execute()` makes the code simple and obvious as it has only one meaning.

Your DB class's `mysqli()` function can use a static class variable to hold its database connection handler. This improves performance by allowing all your classes to do their queries using a single database connection instead of having to make new connections for each query or query group.

16.
Write stupidly obvious code

The number one priority of your team should be code sustainability, and achieving this requires rewarding code quality rather than the speed at which a programmer pumps out code and dumps it on the rest of the team.

Readability should be the main objective of your team. Without readability, the intellectual overhead of your project increases until it reaches the point where adding a simple feature requires having to reverse-engineer a thousand lines of code to understand what on earth was going through the head of the writer of the code.

Put readability above performance. If it takes two database queries to do something in a simple way which can be done with one single complicated query, do the simple query instead and take the performance hit. In 99% of cases readability provides much better results to the project than clever, unreadable, but faster code.

Teach yourself and your team to write stupid code instead of clever code. Clever code almost always means unreadable code, or code that is easy to understand for 50% of your team and unreadable to the rest.

The code below seems really clever and satisfying to a certain type of programmer, especially beginners:

```php
<?php
if($user_id = User::createUser($args)) {
    $new_user = new User($user_id);

    // stuff
}
```

```
?>
```

The code creates a new user in the system, stores the new user's id in **$user_id**, then uses it to initialize a new object for use. The problem is that usually if statements are used to check if something is equal to something else, they are not used for assignment. Using **if** clauses for assignment gives a potential double-meaning to every **if** statement in your project, so that every member of your team will suffer the added intellectual overhead of having to read **if** statements extra carefully to find out whether this is a real **if** or a fake **if** that is doing a job it is not meant to do.

If you simplify the code as follows, a reader can easily read through it without having to pause and go back a line or two to understand what is going on, as everything follows smoothly in a straight line:

```php
<?php
$new_user_id = User::createUser($args);
if($new_user_id) {
    $new_user = new User($new_user_id);

    // stuff
}
?>
```

The difference between the two examples is that first one requires a higher-order understanding of the code. First, you need to understand the obvious meaning of the code, next, your brain needs to use this understanding *to retrieve additional data from your brain* so that it can understand the implied meaning of the code. This double-thinking process might be easy to do it a few times, but if every part of your codebase requires this ridiculous process, you will find that you start to suffer from mental overload very fast.

The second example doesn't require a double-thinking process. *The obvious meaning of the code is the actual meaning of the code.* There are no implied meanings.

Implied meanings create a knot in the code, a break in the follow of your reading. They require you to load data from your brain's long-term storage into your brain's RAM, a process that gets more difficult and fatiguing the more you repeat it and the more complex the code is. By enforcing that there are no implied meanings, that your code is stupidly obvious, you will enable faster reading, faster understanding once you read the code again months later, and easier debugging.

Yes, writing stupidly obvious code requires more lines. But this is not the 1970's, you don't save money by forcing your code into 10 lines instead of 15. You waste money by increasing the number of man-hours needed to maintain and update the code. With modern IDE's, it is quite easy to search throughout your codebase for anything you are looking for, so having longer lines of code almost never impacts your productivity (unless the code is badly written, but that is another issue).

17.
Have a sensible includes policy

Includes simplify your life by making it easy to place the same code block into various files. This is especially useful for templating, as you can have the same headers, navigation bars, sidebars and footers on many different pages.

But they can also exact a very high maintenance cost. Includes, when badly used, make it extremely difficult to edit code without things breaking, as you do not know which variables are going in and which variables are coming out. Imagine a situation like this on **index.php**:

```php
<?php
$variable_one = $something;
$variable_two = $something_else;

include '/footer.php';
?>
```

And then **footer.php** itself is like this:

```php
<?php
$variable_three =
SomeClass::getSomething($something);
foreach($stuffs as $stuff) {
  // lots of stuff
}
include '/footer_part_a.php';
include '/footer_part_b.php';
```

```
?>
```

This creates the typical debugging/maintenance nightmare that by now should be familiar. Making a change to index.php requires you to also review footer.php, footer_part_a.php and footer_part_b.php to ensure that they do not break (for example if footer_part_b.php is using a variable defined on index.php, renaming or deleting the variable on index.php will obviously break some functionality on footer_part_b.php).

The above situation creates a murky soup of variables floating around the files where you never know what is being used where, especially if the files are large.

There are two solutions to these problems that will enable you to enjoy the benefits of includes without suffering the nasty consequences. The first one is to have special HTML-printing classes. For example, you can have a Footer class with a number static functions who perform the jobs that the include files were performing earlier. With this, the bottom part of index.php can look like this:

```
<?php
$variable_one = $something;
$variable_two = $something_else;

Footer::render($args);
?>
```

And the Footer class can look like this:

```
<?php
class Footer {
    public static function render($args) {
        // do stuff

        Footer::renderPartA($args_a);
```

```
        Footer::renderPartB($args_b);
    }

    public static function
renderPartA($args) {
        // do stuff
    }

    public static function
renderPartB($args) {
        // do stuff
    }
}
?>
```

This ensures that you know exactly what is going into the footer-rendering code so that you edit `index.php` without having to look at any other pages to make sure things don't break, you will stay on `index.php`, look at the line of code that says `Footer::render($args);` and make sure the `$args` variable hasn't been deleted, or if renamed, make sure to update the name on this line too.

The second solution is to enclose all of the contents of the included file in a function, and call the function outside of the file. For example, on `index.php` you can have:

```
<?php
$variable_one = $something;
$variable_two = $something_else;

print_footer($args);
include '/footer.php';
?>
```

And inside `footer.php`, you can have:

```php
<?php
function print_footer($args) {
    // stuff

    print_footer_part_a($args_a);
    include '/print_footer_part_a.php';

    print_footer_part_b($args_b);
    include '/print_footer_part_b.php';
}
?>
```

Or this:

```php
<?php
function print_footer($args) {
    // stuff

    print_footer_part_a($args_a);
    print_footer_part_b($args_b);
}

function print_footer_part_a($args) {
    // stuff
}

function print_footer_part_b($args) {
    // stuff
}
?>
```

By enforcing a convention that everything in an included file be surrounded by a function, and all the variables the function needs passed to it as arguments, you can be sure that the include file is not using some random variable on the parent page.

The first method seems like better practice to me, as it completely separates your template parts from your pages, which prevents lazy practices like using a function in an include file that was defined in the parent file, which means the included file cannot actually be included in any other page without also copying that function into the new parent page.

Therefore a total ban on include files (except for the bootstrap file) might be the best practice for ensuring that no member of the team can make lousy use of them. You can force everyone to use classes, which are automatically loaded by the autoloader where they are needed, so that you don't have to worry about file paths.

However, one issue is that not everyone is comfortable with using classes to print out HTML. Therefore you will have to talk to your team and find out what most of you are comfortable with.

Includes are a useful tool when properly used, and when badly used can be a drag on everyone's productivity. Since you cannot trust everyone to use them properly, you need a strongly enforced policy to ensure sense and sensibility.

18.

Use comments to document business decisions and detect badly written code

Here is some good old bad commenting:

```php
<?php
// set faster shipping speed for zip code
45222
if(45222 === $zip_code) {
    $default_shipping_speed =
Shipping::NEXT_DAY;
}
else {
    $default_shipping_speed =
Shipping::TWO_DAY;
}
?>
```

It is obvious from the code that a faster shipping speed is being set for zip code 45222, so there is no need for the comment, which merely repeats what the code is saying. Well-written code makes comments like this completely unnecessary. A good comment would tell you the business reason why a faster shipping speed is being given to this zip code:

```php
<?php
```

```php
// set faster shipping speed for zip code
45222
// because we have a shipping center there
// so we can cheaply ship stuff there
quickly
if(45222 === $zip_code) {
    $default_shipping_speed =
Shipping::NEXT_DAY;
}
else {
    $default_shipping_speed =
Shipping::TWO_DAY;
}
?>
```

Comments that explain the business side of things, for example why certain zip codes, students, schools, file types, domains, etc. are being given special treatment, are extremely important, because a year or two later most people may have forgotten why such a decision was made, and someone may decide to revert it not knowing that it will break certain things. New programmers will have no way to know what is going on with the code unless they ask a programmer who has been working there for a while, who too may have forgotten what is going on, so the issue is escalated to management, who may take days figuring it out. This can be extremely frustrating as one silly clause in the code can hold up a programmer for hours, even days.

There are times, however, that a certain piece of code is so complicated that you know it will be very hard for others to figure out what it is doing, so you feel compelled to write a comment. This often means that the code is too clever and that it should be re-written to make it simpler. This can be painful to do as you may not want to let go of some elegant beauty you have created (which, of course, will be seen by many others as some hairy monster). Hopefully you and your team mates have the self-control to do what is best not what is cleverest. And if you do feel an overpowering urge to signal your reproductive fitness to the

opposite sex by showing off the size of your brain, do leave a good
comment explaining what you are doing.

One type of code that usually requires a comment and cannot be
simplified is regular expressions. For example, what is this JavaScript
code doing?

```
$(this).html($(this).html().replace(/(<p><\/
p>)*\s*$/, ''));
```

Here is the same code when written by a sensible person:

```
//removes empty p tags at the end of the
editor's content area
$(this).html($(this).html().replace(/(<p><\/
p>)*\s*$/, ''));
```

You might be able to figure out what it is doing if you spend 15-30
seconds thinking about it. Those are 15-30 seconds of your life that you
are never getting back. Putting this mental tax on everyone who reads
your code is simply malignant wickedness.

Another type of code that usually require comments are SQL queries,
which are like mini-programs inside your program. It can sometimes
be very hard to understand what a query is trying to do, a comment can
help clarify the purpose without forcing the programmer to test out the
query themselves.

Within SQL queries, **ORDER BY** clauses often require comments,
because sometimes certain pages rely on a very specific order to work
properly, and because. Imagine writing a function that gets the data for
this page, then another coder comes along and decides to reuse the
function for another page, which requires a different order. So, being
short-sighted and caught in the moment as humans are, they change
the order and break the older page.

GROUP BY clauses are even more dangerous, since they fundamentally
change the results returned by a query. Making a change to a **GROUP
BY** is tantamount to writing a whole new query, so they always require

a comment to tell your future self and other programmers why you are grouping things in a particular way.

You can use SQL's comment syntax right inside the query, as follows:

```php
<?php
$statement_rows = DB::getRows("SELECT id
FROM db.statements WHERE date >= ?
# order below is used by statements.php to
# show  data in reverse chronological order
ORDER BY id DESC", $since_date);
?>
```

19.
Class methods must return the ID of business objects they create

Imagine a situation like this:

```php
<?php
class Student {
    public static function
createStudent($args) {
        Assert:: ... // check arguments for
validity

        DB::insert( ... ); // insert the
user into the db
    }
}
?>
```

Such a function will be used like this:

```php
<?php
foreach($imported_data_rows as
$imported_row) {
    $args = [$imported_row[...], ...];

    Student::createStudent($args);
```

```
    // now I need to do something to this
newly
    // created student. Maybe I should do a
    // query like this:
    $new_student_id = DB::getRow('SELECT id
FROM db.students ORDER BY id DESC LIMIT
1')['id'];

    $student = new Student($new_student_id);

    // do stuff with $student
}
?>
```

The issues with the above code should be obvious. You are doing an unnecessary query to get the new student's ID when the creator function could have returned it. And writing unnecessary code creates more chances for bugs, and it exacts a maintenance cost. And, you are not 100% guaranteed to get the ID of the student you just created, if by some remote chance some other code is also running that is creating new students.

Instead, make it a rule that every function that creates business objects should return the ID of the newly created object:

```
<?php
class Student {
    public static function
createStudent($args) {
        Assert:: ... // check arguments for
validity

        return DB::insert( ... );
    }
}
```

```
?>
```

By putting a return before `DB::insert()`, you will be returning the value returned by `DB::insert()`, which should be the ID of the row (and thus the ID of the student) just inserted by it. Now, you can do this instead of the previous loop:

```php
<?php
foreach($imported_data_rows as
$imported_row) {
    $args = [$imported_row[...], ...];

    $new_student_id =
Student::createStudent($args);

    $student = new Student($new_student_id);

    // do stuff with $student
}
?>
```

If you are using MySQLi, you can use the **$mysqli->insert_id** property to get the ID of the row you just inserted into the database.

20.
Do not use echo with HTML if you can help it

The problem with echoing out HTML is that it makes it quite hard to modify the code after it's been written. The following code will be utterly miserable to update, and good luck changing the HTML without breaking it:

```php
<?php
echo '<div><span class="name">' .
$student_first_name
     . ' ' . $student_last_name . '</span>'
     . '<span class="grade">' . $grade .
'</span>'
     . '</div>';
?>
```

The following is prettier, easier to read, and easier to maintain:

```php
?>
<div>
    <span class="name"><?=
$student_first_name ?></span>
    <span class="grade"><?= $grade ?></span>
</div>
<?php
```

If your PHP programmers can't write sensible HTML, they shouldn't be PHP programmers. Note that I'm using the special PHP syntax <?=

`$variable ?>` which prints out the contents of the variable without requiring an **echo**. This makes your code even more readable.

21.

Use an IDE to enforce code style rules (and enhance productivity)

I used to be suspicious of IDE's in the past as they seemed like an unnecessary clutch. Being a staunch individualist, I don't care if everyone else is using something, I won't use it unless it has a proven utility. Once I got familiar with an IDE, I realized that in this particular case, the crowd was right, IDE's *can* offer significant value.

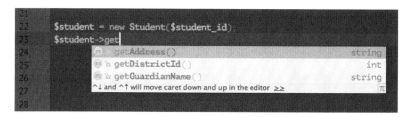

In an IDE I can do a Command + Click on any function name and immediately be taken to the place where it was defined. I can instantiate an object and as I type `$object->get`, get a list of all of its available methods suggested to me, helping avoid having to look at the class to get the correct spelling of the function:

But one of the most valuable features of the IDE is enforcing styling conventions. On the next page is a screenshot of my IDE's styling settings. Every one of my team members has the same styling settings, so that the IDE automatically enforces the rules (and if someone does write code that is not according to the rules, a simple Command + Option + L automatically re-styles the code to fit our conventions.

Having consistent code formatting is important as it enhances the readability and predictability of the code, reducing the mental effort required to understand it.

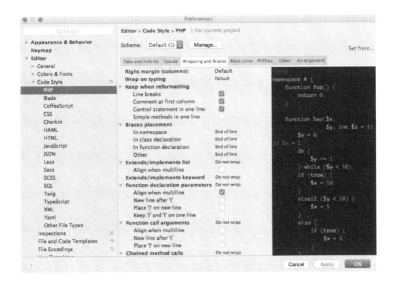

The above screenshots are from PhpStorm on a Mac, but all PHP IDE's probably have similar features. I use Ubuntu Linux at home but my job provides and requires that we use Macs, so my PhpStorm installation is on the Mac.

On an IDE I can do a quick search of my entire codebase for all usages of a particular function, and then have a listing of all the files in a sidebar to work on them one by one. This is more useful than doing a `grep -r` of the root directory, as the list doesn't go away as you work on it, so you don't need to write down a list of files that need to be reviewed and then manually removing the files one by one as they are reviewed.

Another important feature the various other auto-completion and auto-correction facilities the IDE provides, which help me avoid annoyances like making a typo in a variable or function name, or trying to use a private function in a public context without realizing it. The IDE will underline the usage of a private function in red to show the mistake, and the autocomplete will not suggest private functions where they cannot be used.

So IDE's are certainly a clutch. Personally I'm a VIM guy and I am suspicious of anything that tries to do too much cleverness as it often gets in the way. But in this rare case, the overhead added by an IDE is worth it, as it is doubly offset by the productivity enhancements it offers.

22.
Entities enslave your codebase to the database, do not use them

Entities are a very clever idea. Let's say you have a `Student` class. In your database, you can have a table called `student`. Now, let's say you want to get the first name of one of the people in this table. Instead of having to create function like `$student->getFirstName()`, you can do `$student->get('first_name')` (or something similar) and the class automatically retrieves data from the `first_name` column of the `student` table.

So an entity is a row from the database that can walk and talk.

This seems quite handy and easy to use. And it is, if you are writing something that takes a week to write and never plan to update the code again. However, if your project is something long-term and requires collaboration between teammates (as most projects are), then entities are quite a bad idea for many reasons.

The fundamental reason why entities are bad is that once you use entities, you are no longer doing object-oriented programming. You are doing something that looks object-oriented, but it is not. The whole point of object-oriented programming is to make your pages independent of your data structures. The correct rendering of a user's name in the sidebar should not rely on whatever name you choose for the first name and last name columns of the table in the database. Object-oriented programming is about creating classes that provide a reliable, long-term API that all of your code can use knowing that regardless of what changes are made to the class or the database, the API will continue functioning is normal.

This reliable long-term API is the major breakthrough concept of object-oriented programming. This is what object-oriented programming is all about. By using entities, you are using object-oriented functionalities of your programming language to do something completely unrelated to object-oriented programming.

When you use real object-oriented programming, you know that all data retrieved from the database first pass through an intelligent and living class that can do whatever needs to be done on the data, and perhaps retrieve data from multiple sources to create a final product, before the data is returned for use by the client page. Entities turn your classes into nothing but mere tubes through which data passes.

If one day you decide to change things so that you use a different table structure, or perhaps you use something other than SQL-based databases, you will have to update not just your classes, but your entire codebase, since the your table structure is deeply integrated into every part of your codebase. Your database will turn into a massive tentacled Kraken that holds your entire codebase hostage. You will not be able to implement any big new ideas you may have about rearranging your data structures because the Kraken's tentacles will be everywhere.

And it gets worse. Imagine if your database is controlled by a database administrator that is not on your team. That guy can easily become the bane of your existence as every change to your data structures will require his approval. And if he is incompetent he can easily break parts of your project once or twice a month as he makes changes that seem completely logical to him.

So entities make your life easier in the here and now, but they extract a heavy ultimate price in return. Using proper object-oriented programming puts you in charge of your data and gives you the freedom to do what you need when you need it regardless of your DBA's mood and competence.

23.
Use succinctly verbose variable and function names

There is a trend among certain programmers where they think using short variable and function names will earn them medals. My rule is that variable and function names should be verbose enough to remove all ambiguities, but not more verbose. Imagine the following case:

```php
<?php
$students = Student::getStudents();
?>
```

Many programmers will not see anything wrong with the above. But it contains a very annoying ambiguity that creates unnecessary mental load. It requires you to remember what type of data is actually returned by the function, and the `$students` variable in turn, when you eventually use it, requires you to remember what type of data it contains. Is it an array of IDs, of database rows, or of objects?

Of course, if you take 30 seconds to read the rest of the code, and perhaps check out the function definition, you will find out what data is returned by the function. But, as I've said before, that's 30 seconds of your life wasted.

Life gets so much simpler when you bother to make your variable and function names a little more expressive:

```php
<?php
$student_ids = Student::getStudentIds();
```

```php
?>
```

Now, when you read the code, you don't need to hold any metadata in your brain RAM to be able to understand it. The code holds its own metadata through expressive variable and function names.

Here are three more examples, with a too short name given first and its better longer version given on the next line:

```php
<?php
# function name too short
$student_ids =
Student::getStudentsInDistrict($district);
$student_ids =
Student::getStudentIdsInDistrict($district_i
d);

# variable name too short
$rows = DB::getRows(...);
$instructors_in_district_rows =
DB::getRows(...);

# function name too short
$instructor->delete();
$instructor->deleteAccount();
?>
```

There is no need to go overboard and name `$student_ids` as `$student_ids_array` since the plural "ids" suggests that it is an array. Sometimes, however, it is necessary to specify the data type too. For example `$student->getAddress()` is better rewritten as `$student->getAddressStr()` if it returns a string or `$student->getAddressPartsArray()` if it returns different components of the address as an array, since it is not immediately clear what is meant by "address" alone. And instead of having `$user-`

>getPhoneNumber(), use $user->getPhoneNumInt() and $user->getPhoneNumWithDashes(), depending on the type of data the function returns.

24.
Keep intellectual overhead to a minimum by rejecting cool frameworks

The are various frameworks on the Internet that supposedly make it easier to do database queries, or to use objects, or create large-scale web applications. All of these offer some value to some people, but it is a very, very unwise decision to use one just because "everyone else is using it."

If some framework seemingly offers productivity-enhancements of 20% over your current practices, that will almost certainly be offset by inefficiencies and annoyances that you do cannot recognize until you have used the framework for months. Any by that time, if you have already moved everything over to use the next framework, it will be too late to go back.

Another issue is that not everyone on your team will be equally motivated to do things according to the new framework. You may have some tired old programmers who know everything about the business and who will greatly suffer from having to re-learn to do everything in a new way. Of course, younger programmers may think that if you aren't willing to learn, you shouldn't be working as a programmer. But catering to the short-sighted bravado of the youngest members of the team is not the best way to run a project that can last half a decade or more. What actually happens when you enforce a new framework is that a few people will eagerly embrace it, some people will try to learn and after 6 months they start to like the new way of doing things, and the rest will do their best to get away with doing things the old way.

Another issue is that the farther you stray away from bare-bones PHP, the steeper the learning curve becomes for new people who join the team. You can no longer hire someone who is just a good PHP programmer, they will also have to know Pinto and Garbaje. If they don't, it can take them months to get adjusted to the system and start contributing code. But if you stay with bare-bones PHP, new teammates will only need to learn a page or two of conventions, and from there they can immediately start jumping into the system, contributing and getting used to the business side of things.

As a rule of thumb, assume every major framework comes at a productivity cost of 70%, i.e. it reduces the productivity of your project by 70% over the project's lifetime, due to forcing team members to learn to use it, creating a steeper learning curve for new hires, and containing unknown downsides and inefficiencies that may only become apparent after months of usage. If the potential benefits offered by the framework significantly outweigh these costs, then it may be worth a try. Otherwise, stay away from it.

If some major framework or other process change offers a 150% productivity improvement and you cannot see any major downsides, still assume a productivity cost of 70%. What remains is a productivity gain of 80%, meaning that moving onto the new framework or process might make sense.

If you work in a team, have every team member write the productivity gain they expect from moving onto the new framework, allowing them to put negative numbers as well. If you and two other colleagues are working on a project, you could all write down the expect productivity gain as follows:

You: 150%
Colleague A: -10%
Colleague B: 100%

Now, take 70 out of each person's percentage, as follows:

You: 150% - 70% = 80%
Colleague A: -10% - 80% = -90%
Colleague B: 100% - 70% = 30%

And now, average the three resulting numbers:

$(80 + (-90) + 30) / 3 = 20 / 3 = 6.66\%$

This means that your team as a whole believes moving onto the new framework, accounting for all the trouble that it will cause, will still create a productivity gain of 6.66%. This may or may not be worth the move. One of your teammates (the one who put -90%) doesn't like moving to the framework, so in many cases keeping that colleague happy will add more value to the project than moving to the framework, even if their dislike for the framework is stupid. Their dislike could affect their motivation levels for months on end, significantly harming the project.

If, once you average the impressions that all your colleagues have toward a framework, you find out that the expected productivity gain is closer to 50%, then you can be fairly confident that the move will benefit the project.

It is fine to use WordPress for the company's blog, as that is an isolated island and does not affect the rest of your codebase. But making the decision to move everything over to WordPress, Laravel, Symfony, Twig or Silex is a wholly different beast and can create much discontent among team members if done for the wrong reasons.

Epilogue

While I have maintained a somewhat sarcastic attitude throughout this book, I'm actually quite thankful for living in a time when it is so easy to build complex and powerful engines to do tasks that would be so difficult to do otherwise.

This book is not a replacement for Code Complete. This book is merely addendum to it that focuses on object-oriented PHP. I recommend that you read Code Complete if you haven't already (and force everyone else to read it as well if you have the authority to do so). You will never be a great programmer if your ideas about best practices comes from just one or two sources. You need to keep reading and learning until you acquire your very own brand of cynicism that helps you stay productive and avoid unnecessary intellectual overhead.

If you found this book useful, feel free to print out or reuse sections of it to create your own conventions document.

Printed in Great Britain
by Amazon